LET'S LEARN FIRST AID

16 quick and fun exercises

by Kingsley Ogedengbe

THIS BOOK BELONGS TO

_____

Contents

Introduction

Keeping young children safe and protected should be a priority for every parent, guardian and child carer, yet research commissioned by the British Red Cross in April 2017, found that **only 5% of adults** had the skills and confidence to carry out First Aid in an emergency situation.

Children and young people (under the age of 25) make up almost a third (30 per cent, 16.6 million) of the population in England (Office for National Statistics, 2016). Children's healthcare needs can be very different from adults — **they can deteriorate very quickly** — which is why it is so important to know what to do in the event of an emergency.

As a father of three young children I decided to take a proactive approach by teaching our children basic First Aid safety skills. This would not only help prevent needless accidents within the home but avoid trips to A&E and doctors' surgeries, and hours spent waiting there. Additionally, it would provide us parents with the peace of mind and reassurance that all three children had the confidence and knowledge of knowing what to do in emergency situations.

This book contains advice and information regularly found in publications, manuals and guidebooks from the St John Ambulance, the British Red Cross, the British Heart Foundation, the British Resus Council, the Health and Safety Executive (HSE) and the NHS website, plus various other UK health advisory bodies.

It is important that you do not see any of the advice, guidelines or tips contained within this book as a substitute for seeing your regular health advisor or doctor, or calling the NHS number 111 if you are not sure. The information at the time of publication is up to date, however some of the information, practices and procedures may change over time due to new practices, research and findings.

The best way forward to prevent and reduce the numbers of accidents and visits to A&E with young children is to encourage both children and adults to take professional courses in First Aid. I strongly urge you to find a local First Aid class/course to assist with the learning and practice of First Aid. Details of courses for adults and children can be found on *PrimroseFirstAid.co.uk* or *FaskinFirstAid.co.uk*. This book is not intended as a substitute for taking a course with a First Aid course provider.

About This Book

- -

f, like me, you are inspired and motivated to teach your children First Aid safety skills, then I am delighted to introduce you to some easy-to-learn skills and accident prevention tips. I own a regulated First Aid training company and regularly teach First Aid to adults and children. It also helps that my partner is a nurse!

This book aims to bridge the gap of knowledge for both parent/carer and child. It is intended to make the teaching of important life skills easier for parents and carers. All topics have been selected because they are common areas of concern and are useful things to know more about. Each topic is divided into two sections and there is a quiz section at the end of the book.

Learning

This is where you as a parent read to your child, share knowledge, and discuss the topic.

Active Learning / Fun Time

I have tailored this section to give practical fun and enjoyment in teaching your child. Role-playing and performing experiments really works in helping children to remember what they have been learning.

Quiz Time

In this part of the book I ask parents of young children between the ages of 5-7 years to read out questions and help with writing the answers. Children from 8-11 may find the quiz less challenging, and hopefully will be able to read, understand and answer the questions by themselves.

All the answers to the questions are at the back of the book.

On completion of the exercises and quiz, go to the dedicated website at *FaskinFirstAid.co.uk* and get your child a *Faskin First Aid Certificate*.

Tips

- -

Sometimes it can be quite challenging trying to motivate for home learning, especially with multiple children at different ages and stages of development. Having (at the time of publication) three children aged 4, 8 and 10 years (2 girls and a boy) forced me to experiment with different ideas on how to structure the teaching. I advise you to teach each child separately if you can. Here are a few helpful tips.

1 Before you start, think about the child you are going to teach and what the instructional level should be. Try not to push a child beyond their learning capabilities for the sake of teaching one topic. To be effective you may need to separate learning sections.

2 Are you aware of your child's learning ability? To put it simply, there are three common learning styles: visual, auditory and kinesthetic. **Visual** leaners respond well to **seeing pictures**, so try to show as many pictures as possible. **Auditory** learners are **great listeners** — they can understand verbal instructions. **Kinesthetic** learners will benefit from **feeling and touching objects**, so perhaps the Faskin manikin would work well and they would love the Fun Time practicals.

3 Always give praise and encouragement when teaching — children love to hear this and respond positively.

4 Try not to teach all the subjects at once — for young children aged 4-6 years, 15 minutes is enough; for older ones 20 minutes is enough. Each child will develop at a different rate — some have a short attention span, others longer. Be wary not to overload them and drag the lessons and experiments on too long.

5 Last, and most importantly, have fun teaching, playing and sharing knowledge. Even though the topics covered are serious, children learn best when they are having fun.

> **REMEMBER:**
> **The information in this book is to help you to understand important things about staying healthy and happy. However, always remember to see your health advisor or doctor about conditions you are not sure about.**

Faskin, the First Aid Manikin

To help children with learning these topics I have created Faskin the First Aid Manikin.

The name is made up from these parts:

F — FIRST

A — AID

S — SQUAD

KIN — MANIKIN

Faskin's role is to give pointers and tips to children on what to do in the event of an emergency. They can print out a poster or purchase a Faskin manikin.

There is also a Faskin song to help younger ones to learn First Aid. The words are over the page.

You can listen to the song by going to FaskinFirstAid.co.uk

Exercise 1

What is First Aid?

Remember: we should always call a grown-up to help us.

Faskin says:

First Aid is the help you give to someone if they are hurt or feeling very poorly.

Repeat these:

* If someone is **feeling unwell** they will need First Aid
* If someone **falls and hurts themselves** they will need First Aid
* If someone is **upset and crying** they will need First Aid
* If someone is **bleeding** they will need first Aid

Fun Time

It's important to make time to talk with your child and to make this time fun and enjoyable.

Discuss various scenarios with your child about when First Aid should be given.

On a **sheet of paper**, and together with them, write down **10 examples** from school, home and playing outside situations that would need First Aid.

Ask:

● What would they do to **help**?

● Where would they **go**?

● How would they **feel**?

● Ask them if they **remember a situation** where they gave First Aid.

2

The Faskin Song

Who do you call?
Who do you call?

In the case of emergency
Call 999 or 112
In the case of emergency
Call 999 or 112
What do you do
In the case of emergency?
What do you do?
Call 999 or 112

What do you do
When someone else gets hurt?
What do you do?
Sit or lay them down and call for help

Who do you call?
Who do you call?
Who do you call?
Just tell them Faskin the First Aid Manikin

In the case of emergency
Call 999 or 112
In the case of emergency
Call 999 or 112

What do you do
When someone has a bloody nose?
What do you do?
Drop their head down and pinch their nose
What do you do
When someone has an asthma attack?
What do you do?
Sit them down and get their inhaler

Who do you call?
Who do you call?
Who do you call?
Just tell them Faskin the First Aid Manikin

Exercise 2

First Aid Box and Medicine Box

Faskin says:

A First Aid Box is where we put things to treat accidents and emergencies. It contains things for cuts, bleeds, bruises and bumps. Every home, car and school should have a First Aid Box in case of an emergency.

What is contained inside a First Aid Box?

Here is a list of things you can find inside a First Aid Box:

- Sticking Plasters (Band Aids)
- Safety Pins
- Bandages
- Eye Wash
- Gauze
- Scissors
- Wipes
- Gloves
- Eye Dressing
- Triangular Bandage

Fun Time — Introducing the First Aid Box

You will need:

A First Aid Box. If you do not have one you can make one up for now by writing the names on a piece of paper, cutting them out and putting them inside any box.

Show your child your First Aid Box, where it is kept and what is inside.

Here are a few things we must check:

- Always check expiry dates and make a note as to when to replace items.
- Always replace the things you use up.

Faskin says:

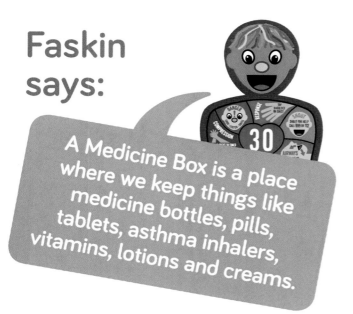

A Medicine Box is a place where we keep things like medicine bottles, pills, tablets, asthma inhalers, vitamins, lotions and creams.

The use of medicines

If a young child finds a **pill** or **sweets** or a **piece of candy**, they *must* give it to a parent or guardian right away. They should **not** taste it first!

Only a parent or guardian should tell a child when they may take medicines and vitamins. They should tell a grown-up right away if they **see other children** getting into medicines.

Parents should put the **child's name** or a **sticker** on their medicine bottle so everyone knows the medicine is theirs.

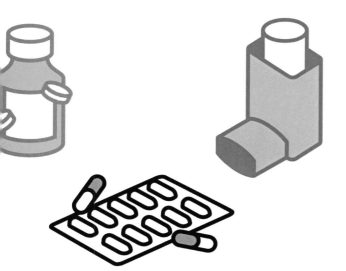

Fun Time — Introducing the Medicine Box

It is very important that you ONLY introduce your child to the Medicine Box when they are over 6 years old and showing interest in the medicines inside the box by asking you specific questions about them. Talking about medicines can help children understand the dangers and the harm they can cause.

Make sure you keep the Medicine Box/Cabinet locked with a key that is kept in a safe place.

Now play the game: When I visited the doctor's

This game can teach a child how to listen and understand what advice doctors give when they visit them at the surgery.

If your child has any medicine, use it; if not, make one up. Don't forget to swap roles!

Start with the sentence: **"When you visit the doctor's surgery, the doctor will say…"**

… [*what medicine you will be using*]

… [*why you need to use it*]

… [*what the medicine does*]

Exercise 3

Dialling for Emergency Services

We are going to learn about how to make a call to the emergency services.
What do we do when there is an emergency?

When do we call for an AMBULANCE?

We call for an ambulance when someone is **very sick**.

We call for an ambulance when someone **cannot move**.

We call for an ambulance when someone is in a **lot of pain**.

When do we call the FIRE BRIGADE?

We call the fire brigade when there is a **fire**.

When do we call the POLICE?

We call the police when we are feeling **very scared**.

We call the police when we need someone to **protect us**.

We call the police when people are **not following the Law** (the rules of the country we live in).

Fun Time Role-Play

Role-play with your child how to make an emergency call on your mobile phone to the emergency services.

Faskin says:

When we call 999/112 for emergency services we will be calling for an ambulance, the fire brigade or the police.

> PLEASE MAKE SURE YOU DO NOT ALLOW YOUR CHILD TO ACTUALLY MAKE THE CALL UNLESS IT IS A REAL EMERGENCY — JUST PRETEND FOR THIS ROLE-PLAY.

- Teach them how to **dial 999/112** on a mobile phone or toy phone.

- Tell them calling 999/112 is **not so scary**.

- Tell them that an operator will ask them **which Emergency Services** they want to speak to. They will then speak to another friendly person from the Emergency Services who will ask them some questions.

- Tell them they need to speak in a **loud, clear voice** and **stay on the phone**.

- Get your child to practise the following:

  - How to say their **full name**

  - The **address or post code** of their home or where they are

  - Telling the person **what has happened**

Did You Know ??

We dial **112** (instead of 999) on our mobile phone to speak with the emergency services when we are not in the UK and are in a European country.

Hygiene and Washing Hands

Bacteria, Fungi and Viruses

These are a group of germs *(imagine a pop group)* that we should know and remember.

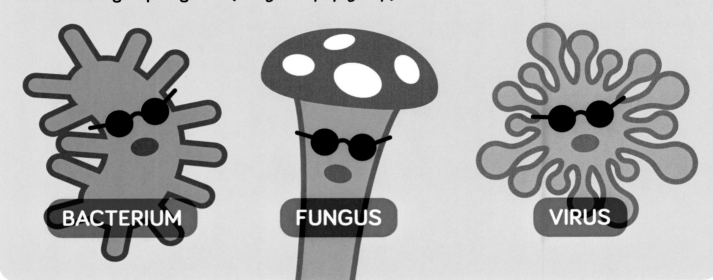

BACTERIUM   **FUNGUS**   **VIRUS**

We can see and smell some bacteria. They can be found in foods, drinks and even in our tummy. Some are known as 'friendly' or 'good' bacteria, others are not and can cause us to be ill.

We can see and smell some groups of fungi and they can grow to be very large. We can eat certain types, like some mushrooms, which taste nice, but there are some that can make us very ill if we eat them.

> Remember, you must always ask the permission of a grown-up before touching or eating mushrooms.

When we come back home from being outside we must wash our hands with soap and water — this will help to stop us from becoming ill and spreading germs.

What do we do when we want to sneeze or cough?

We should always try to sneeze or cough into a tissue and then throw it into a bin. We must always remember to wash our hands afterwards, as this will prevent us passing on our germs. If we do not have a tissue, we should sneeze into our elbow crease.

Fun Time

Faskin says:

By washing our hands with soap we can remove dirt, bacteria, fungi and viruses. This will stop us from becoming ill and prevent us from giving illness to others when we touch them.

Demonstrate by showing or asking your child to wash their hands singing the *Happy Birthday* song twice.

We wash our hands:

- after using the toilet
- before we pick up food to eat, like an apple
- when we get home if we have been playing outside, at school, shopping or visiting somewhere.

Experiment — Pepper, Soap and Water

This shows why it is important to wash hands with soap!

You will need:

- a bowl of water
- ground black pepper
- liquid soap

Sprinkle pepper on the surface of the water. Ask your child to dip a finger inside bowl.

Notice how the pepper sticks to the finger. Remove the finger from water and rinse under the tap.

Spread liquid soap over the finger and dip it into the bowl of water with the pepper again. Watch in amazement how, this time, the finger disperses the pepper.

Explain to your child that we wash our hands with soap to help remove dirt and germs just like pepper.

9

Exercise 5

Minor Injuries, Bumps and Bruises

We can help prevent injuries by being sensible and safe. Here is a list of some things we can do to avoid accidents:

- **Not leaning back** on high chairs.

- Wearing a **helmet** when we ride our bicycles, scooters or skateboards.

- Sitting in a **car seat** designed for children and wearing a **seat belt**.

Try thinking of your own examples of how we can avoid minor injuries.

What do we do when someone hurts their head or has a minor injury?

Think **RICE** :

Rest — Ice — Compression — Elevation

* If someone experiences a knock, bump or blow, **sit them down**, **comfort** them, and make sure they **rest**.

* We can hold a **cold compress** to their bruise (see Exercise 6) — like a bag of ice or frozen peas wrapped in a tea towel — but not for more than **15 minutes** at a time.

* They might need to go to the **hospital** if they become **dizzy** with a **bad headache**.

REMEMBER TO CALL A GROWN-UP AND TELL THEM WHAT HAS HAPPENED. IF THEIR HEADACHE GETS WORSE, OR THEY FEEL SICK, TAKE THEM TO A&E OR CALL 111.

Fun Time Experiment

Faskin says:

Minor injuries are not serious injuries, however if we leave them without treatment they can become serious. We might not need to call for an ambulance when we have a minor injury.

This is a simple way to explain blood flow and why we have bumps and bruises after an accident.

You will need:

- an empty bag/packet (an empty crisp packet will do)
- some sand (enough to fill the packet) or a glass of water if you do not have sand. If you are using water, make sure you do this experiment over a sink or bath.

The sand or water represents blood and the packet represents the skin. If someone receives a blow to the head, a cut or a bruise, then our body reacts by increasing the amount of blood that flows to the affected area.

Now pour the sand/water slowly into the bag. As the bag gets bigger, this represents the swelling up of a bruise. Usually the bigger the injury, the bigger the bruise and the faster the blood will flow to the area. We can show this by increasing how fast we pour.

Faskin says: "Some minor accidents will leave people with small cuts, bruises and bumps."

Bruises can be red in colour and change to a blue/purple and black colour. They can also become swollen and be sensitive to the touch.

Cuts and grazes can sometimes bleed, and they can be a little painful. When we treat cuts and grazes we should wear **disposable gloves** which are found in the First Aid Box/Kit.

Bites and Stings

In the spring and summer there are a lot more insects and plants, so we need to be aware of being bitten and stung.

How to treat a small bite or sting from a plant or insect

1 We first must **tell an adult**.

2 **Scrape off the sting** from the skin using a plastic card-like object such as a credit card.

3 **Wash** with soap and water.

4 Use a **cold compress**, or a pack of frozen peas wrapped in a tea towel, on the area to help slow down the swelling and reduce itching.

5 **Try not to scratch** the area because that will make it worse. If there is pus or the area does not heal, go to see a doctor.

Use tweezers to remove ticks from hair. Wash with soap and water.

If we are allergic to an insect or plant bite or sting we can become very ill quickly. Our lips, eyes and body will swell and our skin might itch. We must call 999/112 and go to the hospital straight away.

If we are bitten by an animal, like a dog for example, we must go to the hospital to see a doctor.

Fun Time

Ask your child if they can think of any insects and plants in your garden/park that sting or bite.

What would they do if they were stung or bitten?

This is a time to hear what your child knows!

Faskin says:

If we get bitten or stung by an insect, plant or animal we should tell a grown-up straightaway. Most bites and stings can be treated at home, but if we are bitten or stung near the mouth, eyes or throat and experience a lot of swelling or find it difficult to breathe we should immediately call 999/112 for an ambulance.

Experiment — How to Make a Homemade Cold Compress to Put on Bites and Stings

You will need:

- a plastic carrier bag
- a tea towel
- some ice cubes

1. Imagine you have been stung or bitten.

2. First, imagine you scrape away the sting using a **stiff card**.

3. Pour ice cubes inside the plastic carrier bag, tie a knot in it to keep the ice cubes in, then wrap the tea towel around the bag. Use this to press down gently on the sore area for **10 minutes** (don't do this for longer as it can cause frostbite).

DRS ABC, which stands for...

Danger—Response—Shout
Airways—Breathing—Compression

- -

This is recommended for children to learn from 7 years upwards.
Try to practise with Faskin Manikin, Faskin Poster, Toy Doll or Teddy Bear.

D — Danger

You should always **look out for danger** so that you do not put yourself at risk of harm, for example from cars if you are helping someone who has been in a road accident, or by **checking for smells** like gas in a house.

R — Response

You can **shake** someone or **tap them** on the chest or shoulders and ask if they are OK.

S — Shout

You should shout **"HELP!"** for a grown-up to come and help. If you are on your own you need to **call 999/112** on a mobile phone.

A — Airways

You can **gently tilt their head up**, lowering their chin towards the ground, to see if there is **anything stuck inside their mouth**.

B — Breathing

You can check to find out if someone is breathing by placing your **ear close to their mouth**. Listen and feel if they are breathing for about **10 seconds**. You can count aloud ("1 and 2 and 3..."). If you suspect **Covid-19** or any other harmful virus on a person, just place a **tissue/light flannel** over their nose and mouth as a check for breath — this also helps minimise contamination.

C — Compression

You can try to **listen to their heart** in their chest. If it has stopped, when help arrives, tell them to **blow 5 breaths** into your friend's mouth and press their **heart 30 times**. Then **2 breaths** and press their **heart 30 times**. They should do this until the ambulance arrives.

If the casualty wakes up and they want to be **sick**, you can help roll them **onto their side**. Keep them on their side until help arrives.

For adults, start with **30 compressions** by pressing at the heart, followed by **2 breaths**. **Continue this sequence** until the medical/ambulance service arrives.

When we press the heart we press down **5 cm (2 inches)** at a rate of **100-120 beats per minute**. Try singing the chorus of the Faskin song to help you with your rhythm!

If you become tired with pressing down, don't forget to **ask for help** to take over.

Fun Time — Let's Role-Play DRS ABC!

The more practice we do, the more confident we become and the less scary it feels.

You can use a Faskin Manikin or Faskin Poster to help remind you of what to do.

You can also practise with your teddy bear or doll.

Hey, grown-ups — it's time to role-play DRS ABC!

Faskin says:

We should try to remember DRS ABC when we find someone lying still and looking very poorly. It is very important you keep yourself safe and always call or send for HELP as soon as possible. Just being there for your friend will really help them feel better and you will be able to say what has happened when an adult or the ambulance arrives.

Bleeding

How we can treat small/light bleeds

Wash the cut under tap water to clean away any dirt.

Cover with a dressing or sticking plaster (Band Aid)

Remember to always try to **wear gloves** and **wash your hands** before and after treatment.

How we can treat big bleeds/wounds

Ask the person who is bleeding to **press firmly down** on the area that is bleeding.

Try to find a **clean cloth** (tea towel, paper tissues, scarf, T-shirt, jumper).

Press down firmly to slow the bleeding.

What to do when someone has an object inside the wound

Sometimes kids can hurt themselves by stepping onto something that sticks into them, like a piece of broken glass or a pin.

Don't pull out the glass or whatever else is stuck in the wound.

You can stop heavy bleeding by **pressing around the wound but not on it** or by putting a pad or clean tissues around the object and bandaging it to **support the object in place**.

Remember to **shout for HELP** and always **talk** to an injured friend to keep them safe.

What to do when someone has a nosebleed

If our nose bleeds because of an accident that has happened to our face, we need to visit a doctor. We can treat a nosebleed by first **sitting down**, taking **tissues** to catch the blood from our nose and **bending our head forwards** — *never backwards*. Hold for **10 minutes**.

This will help to create a **blood clot** (stop the bleeding). Try not to blow your nose for at least **30 minutes**.

Faskin says:

Fun Time

Learning to give First Aid to someone with a cut, graze or small/light bleed

You will need:
First Aid Box that contains
- disposable plastic gloves
- red ink marker pen
- sticking plasters (Band Aids)

Place a small mark on the grown-up's hand, knee, arm or leg with the red ink marker. The person applying the sticking plaster must wash their hands with soap and water before starting treatment, and wear gloves.

Clean the marked 'wound' by running it under the tap with water for 60 seconds. Pat to dry the wound with a clean dressing and place a sticking plaster (Band Aid) over it. Remove gloves and wash hands with soap and water.

Remember, you can find everything you need to treat cuts, grazes and bleeds in the First Aid Box.

Learning to give First Aid to someone who is bleeding a lot

You will need:
First Aid Box that contains
- bandage dressing
- bandage
- red ink marker pen
- disposable plastic gloves

Mark the area you want to treat using the marker. Tell your friend to press firmly on to the 'wound' while you wash your hands and put on gloves. Place the bandage dressing firmly on the wound. If the wound area is on the head, arm or leg you can use a bandage. Wrap the bandage firmly and tie a knot to prevent it loosening. (In reality, we would just keep adding bandages until there was no blood coming through.)

Remember to always ask the injured person to press firmly. If they cannot, you must do it for them. Try also to keep them warm as they may feel cold.

Choking

What do we do if we see someone choking?

We should first encourage them to **cough**. If they are not able to, we can **ask them "are you choking?"** If they nod their head to say "yes" we must **call for help** immediately.

When help arrives, they should give **4 rounds of 5 back blows** in between the shoulder blades, using the flat part of the hand, followed by **5 stomach thrusts** if the object has not come out.

If the object has still not come out then we need to **call the emergency services** for an ambulance. If the person becomes **very still** and **changes colour** we must give them **CPR** (cardiopulmonary resuscitation).

> You should ONLY give stomach thrusts and CPR if you are First Aid trained.

Tips on practising choking safety

- **Chew** all the food in your mouth, thoroughly, before swallowing it.
- Only put **food and drink** in your mouth.
- **Avoid running and eating/drinking** at the same time.

How to perform an abdominal (stomach) thrust on someone who is choking

- Stand behind the person who's choking.
- Place your arms around their waist and bend them forwards.
- Clench your fist and place it right above their belly button.
- Put the other hand on top of your fist and pull firmly and quickly inwards and upwards
- Check to see if object has come out.
- Repeat this movement up to 5 times if necessary.

This procedure is drastic and very powerful — if performed, the casualty MUST visit the hospital for a check-up afterwards.

Abdominal thrust

Fun Time Role-Play

Universal sign for choking, and 5 back blows

You and another person will be needed, to play the First Aider and the casualty.

Role play the universal sign for choking. Decide who is the First Aider and who is the casualty.

The casualty places their **two hands** to cover their **neck** (see image). The First Aider asks the question, "Are you choking?" The casualty is unable to speak and replies by **nodding their head**, yes.

Faskin says:

Sometimes eating and drinking can make us cough — it's OK to cough when we need to. If someone eats or drinks something but cannot cough or make a sound then we need to get help immediately.

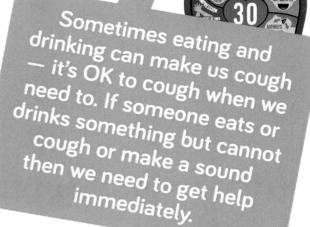

Pretend to **call for help** — in real life, you should do this **immediately** as the situation could be very dangerous.

Practise by **pretending to give 5 back blows** between the shoulder blades.

Universal choking sign

5 back blows

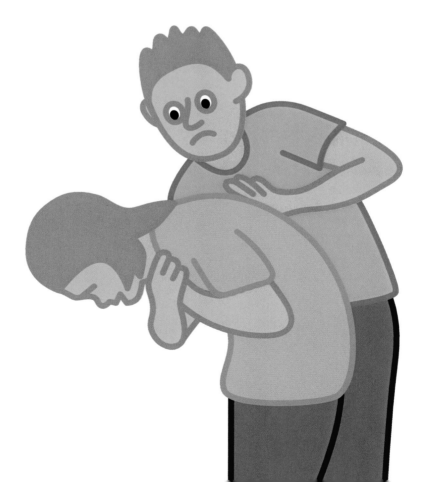

Asthma

Asthma affects many people, from friends in your class to parents, grandparents and other relatives. When someone is having an asthma attack it is important that they receive their inhaler.

What to look out for:

- ✳ **Difficulty breathing** and wheezing sounds.
- ✳ **Coughing** through the night.
- ✳ The feeling of a **tight chest**.

How to be a First Aider when someone is having an asthma attack

Start by asking if they need their **medication** — usually an **inhaler**.

You should give them their medication and **allow them to use it**.

Always check **their name is on the medication** before you give it to them.

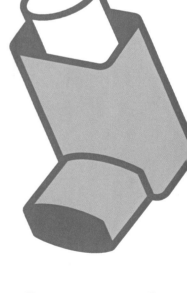

Causes or triggers for asthma attacks:

- Flower pollen
- Cold weather
- Animal hair
- Dust
- Flu or colds
- Cigarette smoke
- Exercise

Fun Time Experiment — Make a Breathing Model

Faskin says:

We cannot see asthma because it is a disease inside our chest that causes our airways to become smaller and makes breathing with our lungs very difficult.

You will need:

- a straw
- some Plasticine or playdough
- 2 balloons
- scissors
- a plastic bottle
- an elastic band

Carefully cut your bottle in half (**this must be done by a grown-up**).

Put the **straw** into the **neck of one balloon** and secure tightly with the **elastic band**, but not so much that you crush the straw. The air must flow through, so **test it by blowing a little** through the straw to make sure the balloon **inflates**.

Put the straw and balloon into the neck of the top half of the bottle and use the playdough to **make a seal** around the straw and bottle neck — make sure you don't break the straw.

4   **Tie a knot** at the bottom of the **second balloon**, then **cut the top off** that balloon and use the bottom section with the knot to **cover the open end** of the bottle.

5   When you **pull the knot** of the second balloon down you will see the first balloon inside the bottle **inflate**. This is how we breathe.

6   When we breathe in through our nose and mouth, air travels down through our airways and into our lungs. When **the straw is squeezed, air cannot pass through** easily. This is just like an **asthma** attack, where people find it **difficult to breathe**. Using medication, like an **inhaler**, helps to ease this breathing difficulty.

Minor Burns and Scalds

There are 5 types of common burns and scalds we should know about:

- Sun
- Fire
- * Chemical
- * Cold/ice
- * Electrical

How do we treat a minor burn or scald?

You should first see that it is **safe** for you and the person you are treating by **keeping far away from fires, chemicals and electricity power sources**. Be prepared as you may need to call the fire brigade and ambulance.

Next, slowly run **cool water** from the tap over the burn area for **20 minutes**. Avoid using an ice pack as this is **too cold**. Then **cover** the burn area with **clingfilm**.

All **jewellery needs to be removed** because it is likely there will be swelling.

The casualty may feel cold, so **wrap up** other areas of the body not affected with **dry, warm clothes**.

Parts of the body like eyes, mouth, nose, ears and private parts need **immediate hospital care**, along with any burns bigger than the size of a **coin**.

DO NOT try to remove clothes stuck on skin — leave that to DOCTORS.

A minor burn or scald can become infected if not treated correctly — always check with your doctor.

Fun Time

Learning how to treat a minor burn or scald

You will need:
- **2 people (adult and child)**
- **clingfilm**
- **red marker pen**

First, decide who will play the First Aider and who will play the casualty.

Mark an area on the **arm of the casualty** with the red marker pen.

The First Aider needs to run the arm of the casualty under a **cool tap** for a **few minutes** (remember, in real life it's 20 minutes).

Then, **gently wrap** the area using **clingfilm**.

Warning: NEVER use clingfilm near your face — instead, use a bandage dressing from a First Aid Box. Wrap around twice.

Faskin says:

It is better to avoid burns and scalds than to have to treat them. Most happen in and around our homes. We should be very careful not to play with things, or around things, that could burn us.

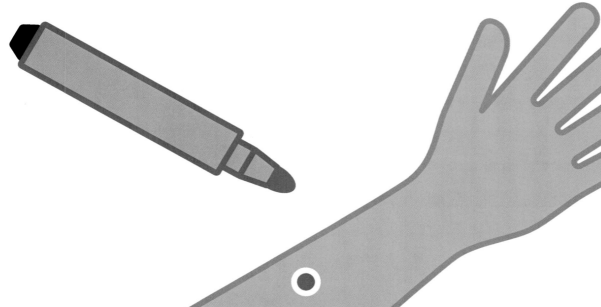

23

Allergic Reactions and Anaphylaxis

There are many things that can cause someone to have an allergic reaction. Often, reactions can be simply treated. But sometimes a person can have a **very serious reaction** which can cause them to become very sick and end up in hospital. We call this **Anaphylaxis** (ana-fil-ax-is).

Here is a list of a few common things that can cause an allergic reaction or anaphylaxis:

- Milk
- Peanuts
- Dust and dust mites
- Animal fur
- Hair
- Insect bites and stings
- Metals
- Medicines
- Pollen
- Fruits
- Soap/Creams

What do we do?

In an allergic reaction we need to act like police detectives and find the **cause** or **triggers**.

If at all possible, remove the casualty as **far away** as you can from the cause/trigger.

If they have a **rash** developing, taking a **cool shower** and applying a **cold compress** on the area will help them.

They should visit their **doctor or pharmacist** for creams, Piriton liquid and tablets.

> If they are regularly suffer with allergic reactions they should see a doctor to be tested.

What is Anaphylaxis?

Anaphylaxis (pronounced ana-fil-ax-is) is a **very serious allergic reaction** to certain foods and drinks and can happen **very quickly**. It can cause **swelling** in the skin, lips, mouth, throat or lower airway, causing difficulty in swallowing and/or breathing.

The cause is when their body **thinks it's under attack** and begins to produce chemicals inside their body to defend it.

People who suffer must **try to avoid triggers** like foods such as peanuts, seafood, shellfish, tree nuts, kiwi fruit, tomatoes.

Certain insect **bites and stings** from bees and wasps could cause a reaction.

Anyone with this condition is aware they must **avoid** these things.

What do we do in an emergency?

Alert a **grown-up** and **call 999/112**.

Sit the casualty down and give **medication**, e.g. Adrenaline Auto-Injector Pen (AAI).

Faskin says:

We are going to learn about allergic reactions and anaphylaxis (ana-fil-ax-is). This can help us understand what to do if we or our friends have an allergic or anaphylactic reaction.

How to spot an allergic reaction (in some people)

* They might feel **tingling** on their lips.
* You might see their face, eyes and lips **swell up**.
* They might begin to **itch** and you might see **spots or a rash** on their skin.
* They might feel **hot and sweaty**.
* They might feel **sick** with **tummy ache**.
* Their eyes might **look like they are crying**.

Fun Time Role-Play

To help you remember how to help someone in an emergency you are going to role-play treating someone who is having an anaphylactic reaction.

You will need:

* **2 people to play — one casualty and one First Aider**
* **a large felt-tip pen *with the top on***
* **great acting skills!**

Decide who is the casualty and who is the First Aider.

The casualty **pretends to eat or drink** something that is a trigger.

Go through the **symptoms**:

* Wheezing
* Coughing
* Pretend to be hot, with a tummy ache, restless and confused

The First Aider needs to **shout for help, call 999/112**, and ask the casualty where their **AAI pens** are kept.

Pretend to inject the casualty in the top of their thigh once.

Broken Bones / Fractures

Did You Know  ???

* Bones are white in colour and made up of **collagen fibres** and **calcium**. They are very strong and help give our bodies support and structure.

* A **fracture** (*frak-ture*) means the same as a broken bone. Young children's bones are 'bendy' so they don't break 'cleanly' — instead they crack, forming a **greenstick fracture**.

* When we are born we have **270 bones** but as we become adults this reduces to **206 bones**, because some of our bones fuse together.

* Although our bones are very strong, some of them — like fingers and toes — can easily be broken.

* It can take up to **3-6 months** for a badly-broken bone to heal.

What do you do if someone has a broken bone?

The treatment will depend upon on **where** the break is and how **serious** it is.

Only treat the casualty in an area that is **safe** — check all around you for danger.

Hairline (*hair-line*) fractures (cracks) are **very small** — you will not be able to see them, but there will be pain and swelling. Put a cold pack on the area for **10 to 15 minutes maximum** at a time (any longer may cause frostbite). Try to do this **every 1 to 2 hours**.

If a **hand/arm** is affected, put it in a **sling** and take the casualty to hospital for **x-rays**.

> More serious or bigger breakages require you to not move the person and to call or send someone for help.

Support the break by placing pillows or jumpers on either side.

If there is **bleeding**, use a **clean dressing cloth** and ask the casualty to apply pressure on it. **Call for help** *immediately* and try not to touch the blood to avoid the possibility of contamination.

Stay with them and offer **kind words**.

Wrap them with a **warm blanket** as they will feel cold.

Fun Time Role-Play

Faskin says:

When a bone has been broken or cracked it is very painful. Sometimes we see blood and a lot of swelling in the area.

You will need:

- Minimum of 2 people (1 casualty and 1 First Aider)
- First Aid Box
- 1 triangular bandage or pillowcase
- Blanket

Let's role-play how to treat a broken arm

1 Check for **danger** and move the casualty *only* if the surroundings are *unsafe*.

2 Check the area of the arm that has been broken to see if it is **deformed** (not the shape it should be) and to see if it is **bleeding**. You can also check to see if there are any **other injuries** by asking and looking.

3 It is important that the casualty **stays still** and does not move their injury.

4 **Call for help** or send someone for help.

5 It really helps to **stay calm** and keep the casualty calm by **explaining** what you are doing to help.

6 **Wrap** the broken arm with a **bandage** (in real life, only a trained First Aider should do this).

7 The casualty may feel **cold** due to **shock**, so cover them with a **warm blanket**.

8 Put the broken arm in a **sling** (see right).

9 Arrange to take the casualty to **hospital**.

Dangerous Liquids and Gases

Did You Know ???

Poisons can be found in liquids we use in the **kitchen, bathroom, toilet** and **garden**. Some poisons can also be found in **bites and stings** from animals, insects and plants. We can **breathe in** poisonous gases through **smoke and fumes** as well.

We should understand there are 4 ways poisons can enter our body:

- **By mouth, drinking**
- **Injection**
- **Absorption —**
  insect or snake bites through our skin
- **Inhalation —**
  breathing in through the nose

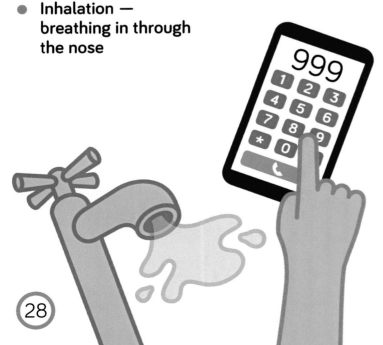

What should we do if someone has been poisoned?

Call for help by dialing 999/112 (ambulance) or **call a grown-up**.

We should **NEVER** give them something to **drink** or try to get them to vomit.

If it's a poison on the skin or in the eye we should **wash it off** under a tap for **20 minutes** with just water.

If we smell poisonous gases we must **run outside** to open fresh air.

We should **NEVER pick up needles or syringes**.

When you go to the hospital **take the container** with the poisonous chemical with you if you can, so they can give the correct treatment.

Fun Time Game

It is important we know and understand what is poisonous in our home, so here is a fun game that can help us understand which things we should *never* play with, eat or drink.

We are going to play 'I-spy'.

How to play

Minimum of 2 players

One player starts by choosing anything they see in a room they think is edible (good to eat) or not edible (bad to eat) and the other has to guess what it is. Start the sentence with "I-spy…" then name what it is.

Example: "I spy… a bottle of soap."
The other player must reply "not edible" if they are to be right.

This game is helpful in preventing accidents by reminding children what they should not eat or play with.

Faskin says:

Dangerous liquids are known to be poisonous (poi-son-us). They can cause us to become very ill — or even die — very quickly. We must be very careful not to play with these liquids.

The Recovery Position

Did You Know ???

We can put children, from 1 year (12 months) upwards, and adults, into the Recovery Position. **Those younger than 12 months must be carried differently** and **pregnant mums** rolled on the **left side only**.

What does unconscious mean?

When we are awake, with our eyes open and able to think and talk we are **conscious**. But if we are asleep and breathing and cannot be woken up easily then we can be **unconscious**.

Sometimes people become unconscious when they accidentally fall and hit their head.

When should we roll someone into the Recovery Position?

If an emergency situation arises we should first remember **DRS ABC**. If they are breathing and we are waiting for help we can roll them into the **Recovery Position** (see Exercise 7).

We DO NOT roll somebody into recovery if we think they have a serious injury to their neck and back.

If someone has had a **seizure** (fit), it may be safer for them to be rolled into the Recovery Position.

Why not think and discuss situations where you would consider rolling someone into the Recovery Position?

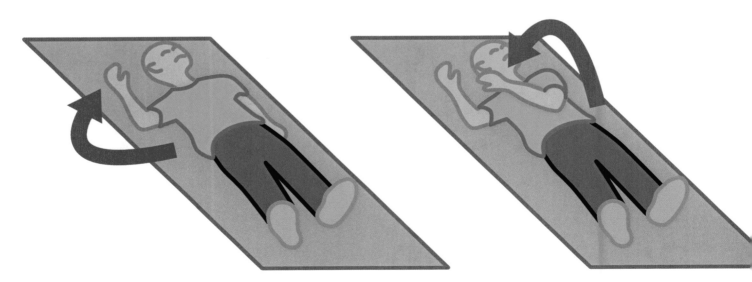

Fun Time

Faskin says:

If a person is unconscious (un-con-chus) and breathing with no other issues that can affect their life, you can put them in the Recovery Position. Putting them in the Recovery Position will keep their airway clear and open. It also helps avoid them choking from any vomit or fluid.

Teaching your child how to put someone into recovery is really simple and easy to learn, and it could help save a life.

You will need:

- **a space to roll**
- **a pillow or mat to roll on if you are on hard floor**

How to put someone into the Recovery Position

1 **Kneel** beside them (it can be left or right).

2 If they are bleeding, always roll onto the **side that they are bleeding from**.

3 Place the arm **closest** to you at a **right-angle**.

4 Bring the arm **furthest** from you **across their face.**

5 Bend the **knee furthest** from you and cross the **bent leg over the straight leg**.

6 **Roll over** from bent elbow and bent knee **all at once**.

7 Move the **knee up** to prevent them from rolling backwards.

8 Adjust their **head up** to allow easy breathing.

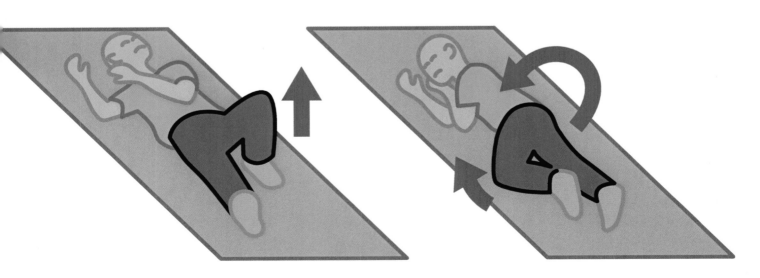

AED — What It Is and How to Use It

If an adult or child is not responsive to our call or touch, and is not breathing, we need to do four things:

1 Shout for help from an adult.

2 Make sure an ambulance is on its way.

3 Assist, if needed, with CPR (see Exercise 7).

4 Ask someone to find, and bring back, an AED.

AED stands for Automated External Defibrillator. This is an electronic device that is able to check someone's heart rhythm to see if a shock is required. **If a shock is needed, the machine will say something like "Shock is advised".** The device will then help us apply an electric shock through pads which we place on the casualty — this can help their heart recover.

We can find AEDs in many public places like train stations, telephone boxes, shopping centres, supermarkets and even in some schools. To find an AED, we should **look for the special AED symbol.**

How to use an AED

Once the AED arrives we must switch it on. We will hear a voice, which will ask us to connect the pads to the casualty's chest. When we are treating a casualty, we should place the pads on the **bare chest** (not on clothing).

If the casualty is an adult, we place one pad on the right side of their chest (our left, as we face them) and the other on the left side of their rib cage (see diagram). If they are a child, we place one pad on their chest and the other on their back.

Once we have placed the pads on the chest we must NOT touch the casualty. The AED will analyse the heart rhythm and advise us if the casualty requires a shock. The AED might say something like "Shock advised, please stay clear". Once the light on the button starts to flash, we can press it.

After that, we continue with CPR, with cycles of 30 compressions and 2 breaths, until the machine asks us to stop, or the medics arrive.

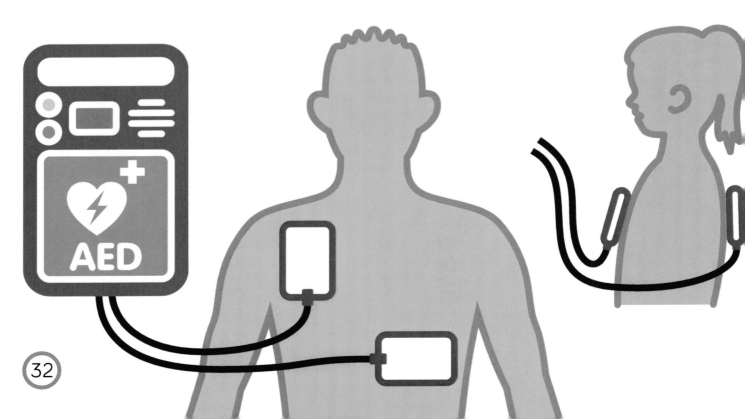

Faskin says:

By using an AED, we can hugely increase someone's chances of survival and recovery, much more than by using just CPR.

Fun Time

Let's make a 'pretend AED' out of paper, and practice using it.

You will need:

- **2 people (or you and a *Faskin* manikin!)**
- **2 sheets of A4 plain paper**
- **2 pieces of string, each 30cm in length**
- **Marker pens**
- **Sticky tape**
- **Double-sided sticky tape**

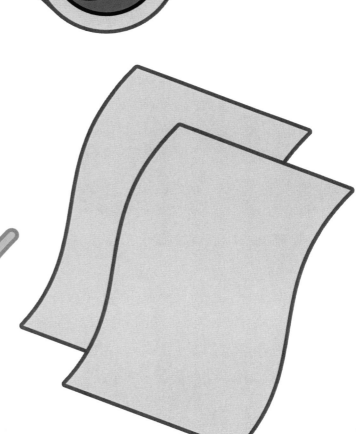

Take one A4 piece of paper, mark out the word '**AED**', and draw a button. Tear the other sheet of paper in half to make two pads. Mark the letters 'L' (for left) and 'R' (for right). Attach a piece of string to each pad and then to the AED. Place some double-sided tape on the underside of the pads, so they will stick on.

Lay the 'pretend casualty' on the floor, then apply the pads onto them in the positions shown in the diagram.

Say **"Stand back, shock advised"** and press the pretend button on your AED. Then, continue with CPR (see Exercise 7).

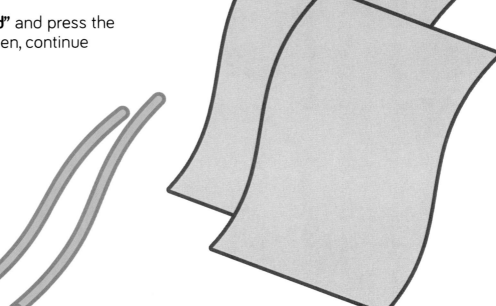

33

Homemade First Aid and Coronavirus 'Survival' Kit

This is quick and easy to make at home for your child, and it's particularly useful for them to take to school, and on day outings.

You can adjust the contents to suit your child's needs.

You will need:

- 1 pair of plastic gloves
- 1 small hand sanitiser
- 1 facemask
- 1 tissue
- 1 antiseptic wipe
- 1 sticky plaster
- 1 small container

Place items in a sturdy plastic container and mark your child's name on it.

Safety at Home

- -

Faskin wants you all to be safe, and feel safe, at home!

★ Emergency safety check — FIRE ALARMS IN ALL ROOMS NEED TO BE CHECKED ★

1 Try to remember your **full name**, and the **address where you live**.

2 Never play around the **kitchen** area while there is **cooking** going on.

3 Never play with **cigarette lighters**.

4 Never touch or play with **poisonous liquids**.

5 Never play with **hot electrical items** like **irons**, **toasters** or **hair straighteners**.

6 Never take any **medicine** without parents or carers knowing.

7 Always keep the **First Aid Box well stocked**.

8 **Chew foods slowly** and **don't run or try to speak** when you are eating.

9 Always be in reach of a **mobile phone** in case you need to call.

10 Remember and practise how to **call 999/112**, and what to say.

Useful Organisations

- -

NHS Helpline

Tel: 111

NHS Website

nhs.uk

Police non-emergency number

Tel: 101

Anaphylaxis Campaign

anaphylaxis.org.uk
Tel: 01252 546100

Asthma Society

asthma.org.uk
Tel: 0300 222 580

Resuscitation Council

resus.org.uk

Primrose First Aid Training

Details on paediatric courses
PrimroseFirstAidTraining.co.uk

Faskin the Manikin
To find out more, visit *FaskinFirstAid.co.uk*

Glossary

AAI Pen

Adrenaline Auto-Injector Pen, used to treat anaphylactic reactions.

Adrenaline

Also called Epinephrine, this is a substance the body makes that has effects like increasing blood flow and air flow.

Allergy

When a person's body reacts to something from outside it like food, a chemical or a sting.

Anaphylactic Reaction (Anaphylaxis)

Like an allergy but more serious and dangerous, with the effects often happening very quickly.

Asthma

A disease of the lungs that makes it difficult to breathe.

Bacterium (plural: Bacteria)

A microscopic (very, very tiny) organism that plays a part in the decay of living things.

Blood Clot

When blood becomes less liquid and forms a solid lump.

Calcium

A soft, white substance that is found in rocks and also helps build healthy bones and teeth.

Casualty

A person who is injured or unwell.

Cold Compress

A cool, wet cloth or bag of chilled or frozen material used to help reduce swelling and discomfort.

Collagen Fibres

Protein fibres that help give strength and cushioning to bones and skin.

Compression

Applying pressure to a wound or swelling, often with a dressing or cold compress.

Compressions

Pressing on a person's heart many times, quickly, when it has stopped, to try to restart it.

Conscious

Awake and aware of the things around you; able to feel, think, hear, see.

CPR (Cardiopulmonary Resuscitation)

An emergency procedure that uses chest compressions and breaths when someone's heart and breathing have stopped.

Dressing

A sterile pad or compress applied to a wound to promote healing and protect the wound from further harm.

DRS ABC

Stands for Danger—Response—Shout—Airways—Breathing—Compression (see Exercise 7).

Elevation

Raising a limb or body part to decrease blood flow.

First Aid Box/Kit

A box or bag containing items that can be used to help treat a casualty.

Fracture

A break, usually in a bone.

Frostbite

An injury caused by freezing of the skin and underneath the skin.

Continued overleaf

Glossary (continued)

Fungus (plural: Fungi)
An organism such as a mushroom, toadstool, yeast or mould.

Gauze
A medical fabric with a loose, open weave, which is used in wound care and is commonly made of cotton.

Germ
A microscopic (very, very tiny) organism, especially one which causes disease.

Greenstick Fracture
A fracture of the bone, mostly in children, in which one side of the bone is broken and the other only bent.

Hairline Fracture
Also known as a Stress Fracture, this is a small crack or severe bruise within a bone.

Hygiene
Maintaining health and preventing disease through cleanliness.

Inhaler
A small device for giving a drug which is to be breathed in, used for relieving asthma and other breathing conditions.

Manikin (also Mannequin)
A life-sized human model used in medical education.

Medicine Box/Cabinet
Place where we keep medicines such as pills, tablets, vitamins, lotions and creams.

Pollen
A powdery substance consisting of grains from the male part of a plant which help the plant reproduce.

Recovery Position
A position used in First Aid to prevent choking in unconscious patients (see Exercise 15).

Seizure (or Fit)
A sudden, uncontrolled electrical disturbance in the brain that can cause changes in behaviour, movements and level of consciousness.

Shock
A critical condition brought on by a sudden drop in blood flow, reducing delivery of oxygen and nutrients to vital organs.

Stomach Thrust
Also known as an Abdominal Thrust, this is an emergency technique used to help clear someone's airway.

Symptom
A feeling of illness or physical or mental change that is caused by a disease.

Syringe
A hollow, cylinder-shaped piece of equipment, usually with a needle, used for sucking liquid out of something or pushing liquid into something.

Triangular Bandage
A piece of cloth folded into a right-angled triangle, to cover and/or support a wounded limb or body part.

Trigger
Something that either sets off a disease in people who are prone to developing it, or that causes a certain symptom to occur in a person who has a disease.

Unconscious
Not awake, not aware of the things around you and cannot be woken up.

Virus
A microscopic (very, very tiny) organism that is smaller than a bacterium and cannot grow or reproduce outside a living cell.

This section is where you test what you have learned through all the exercises and experiments in this book, about First Aid and Health & Safety.

Once you have completed ALL the exercises and answered ALL the questions in this quiz section, you can get your answers checked.

Your aim is to get full marks (22). If you have answered any questions wrongly, don't worry — you can get it explained to you so you know what the correct answer is and why that's the answer.

When you have completed the quiz correctly you can get a *Faskin First Aid Certificate*. This will show that you have gained a basic knowledge and understanding of First Aid and that you are a member of *Faskin's First Aid Squad*.

Don't forget to ask for help with any of the questions if you don't understand!

GOOD LUCK!

First Aid

- -

1 ## What is First Aid?

Tick the ONE correct answer from the list below.

A ⬜ Laughing at someone.

B ⬜ A type of fizzy drink.

C ⬜ The help you give to someone if they are hurt or feeling poorly.

2 ## What should she do to avoid an accident?

Look at the image (right), then tick the ONE correct answer.

A ⬜ Run down the steps quickly without holding onto the handrail.

B ⬜ Walk down carefully holding onto the handrail.

C ⬜ Slide down the steps.

Hygiene

- -

3 When we sneeze we should do it into a tissue, or into our elbow crease if we do not have a tissue. We should then wash our hands. What should we do with the tissue we have just used?

Tick the ONE correct answer from the list below.

A ⬜ Put it in the bin.

B ⬜ Put it in our pocket.

C ⬜ Leave it on the table for someone to pick up.

4 Washing our hands with soap and water before we touch food will help to stop us putting germs into our body. Is this true?

Tick the ONE correct answer from the list below.

A ⬜ Yes

B ⬜ No

Head Injuries

5 Small head injuries like a bump or bruise can be treated by doing what?

Tick the ONE correct answer from the list below.

A ◯ By placing a hot sponge on the bruise.

B ◯ By using an ice pack or small bag of cold compress.

C ◯ By massaging the area.

6 A person can experience headaches and feel sick, dizzy and really tired after hitting their head. Is this true?

Tick the ONE correct answer from the list below.

A ◯ Yes

B ◯ No

Unresponsive

7 What should we do if we see someone lying down with their eyes closed?

Tick the ONE correct answer from the list below.

A ◯ Check for danger, check for their response, and call for adult help.

B ◯ Run away and don't tell.

C ◯ Ignore them and walk away.

8 What is the meaning of DRS ABC?

Tick the ONE correct answer from the list below.

A ◯ Dance, Rest, Sing, Airways, Breathing, Call.

B ◯ Danger, Rice, Shout, Airways, Bruising, Circulation.

C ◯ Danger, Response, Shout, Airways, Breathing, Circulation.

Cuts and Nosebleeds

9 **If someone has a small cut or graze from having an accident in the playground at school what should we do?**

Tick the ONE correct answer from the list below.

A ⬜ Ignore them and continue playing.

B ⬜ Tell them that we can help by taking them to the duty teacher, who will get a First Aid Kit box and treat the wound.

C ⬜ Laugh at them and run away.

10 **If someone is experiencing a nosebleed, they should pinch the soft part of their nose with a tissue and have their head facing downwards. Is this true?**

Tick the ONE correct answer from the list below.

A ⬜ Yes

B ⬜ No

Choking

11 **How do we know when someone is choking?**

Tick the ONE correct answer from the list below.

A ⬜ They will say "I am choking" and stamp their feet.

B ⬜ The person will shout for help and try to call 999.

C ⬜ We should ask them the question, "Are you choking?" If they answer by nodding their head up and down, we know they are choking.

12 **A person who is choking needs 5 Back Blows and 5 Stomach Thrusts; you must do at least 4 rounds of this. Don't forget to call for help from an adult. Is this true?**

Tick the ONE correct answer from the list below.

A ⬜ Yes

B ⬜ No

Asthma

A

13 What is asthma?

Tick the ONE correct answer from the list below.

A ☐ A type of tube that a doctor would use to check your breathing.

B ☐ It's when someone is feeling sick in their stomach.

C ☐ It's when a person's lungs can't take in enough air for them to breathe.

14 What does an asthma inhaler look like?

Pick the ONE correct image from the two images (right).

A ☐

B ☐

B

Burns

15 Burns can be very painful and are caused by a number of things. What could cause a burn?

Tick the ONE correct answer from the list below.

A ☐ Being hit by a football.

B ☐ Putting your fingers in snow.

C ☐ Spilling hot water on your skin.

16 You should run cool water on your skin for 20 minutes when you have a burn from hot water. Is this true?

Tick the ONE correct answer from the list below.

A ☐ Yes

B ☐ No

Allergic Reactions

17 **Some people become very ill and react badly when they eat, touch or smell certain things — if they do, they will need help. What should we do?**

Tick the ONE correct answer from the list below.

A ⬜ Shout for an adult immediately, then ask the person where their medication is kept.

B ⬜ Become scared and run away.

C ⬜ Sit quietly, watch and say nothing.

18 **A person who is suffering with an allergic reaction (sometimes known as an *anaphylactic reaction*) might experience their lips, eyelids and face swelling up. Is this true?**

Tick the ONE correct answer from the list below.

A ⬜ Yes

B ⬜ No

Fractures

19 **If someone has had a nasty fall or accident, how can we tell they might have broken a bone?**

Tick the ONE correct answer from the list below.

A ⬜ If they are able to rub the area without feeling pain.

B ⬜ If they get up without help.

C ⬜ If it hurts to move the limb and there is a big bruise or lump.

20 **We should use an arm sling if someone has broken their leg. Is this true?**

Tick the ONE correct answer from the list below.

A ⬜ Yes

B ⬜ No

Seizures

21 When someone has a seizure, what can happen to their body?

Tick the ONE correct answer from the list below.

A ☐ Their body stays still and does not move.

B ☐ Their body starts to shake and they can clench their fists.

C ☐ They sit down calmly and go to sleep.

22 After someone has had a seizure they become very tired and might want to sleep. Is this true?

Tick the ONE correct answer from the list below.

A ☐ Yes

B ☐ No

WELL DONE

on completing this quiz!

Your final mark is
_____ out of 22.

If you have any of your answers marked wrong, just ask why. Once you have shown that you understand what the right answer is, you can re-mark the answer correct.

Remember — once you have completed the quiz and received a pass mark, an adult can get you your *Faskin First Aid Certificate* at *FaskinFirstAid.co.uk*

Quiz Answers

---

1 C   5 B   9 B   13 C   17 A   21 B

2 B   6 A   10 A   14 A   18 A   22 A

3 A   7 A   11 C   15 C   19 C

4 A   8 C   12 A   16 A   20 B

Made in the USA
Las Vegas, NV
19 January 2024

84565139R00033